AF412433

NAGARJUNA
THE SECOND BUDDHA

Mohini Kent

Foreword by
HH the Dalai Lama

wisdom
tree

First published 2016

Photograph Credits: promienie.net-pp17, 27, 68, 73; tsemtulku.com-pp 10, 20; tobygillies.com-p 64; wikimedia.org/Creative Commons-p 35; Courtesy of the office of HH the Dalai Lama-pp 18-19; Tenzing Choyang Gyari-p 2; Google Art Project/Creative Commons-p 30; Kshipra Simon (Tushita Mahayana Meditation Centre, New Delhi)-p 39; Benjamin Mathews/Creative Commons-p 62; landofenlightenedwisdom.org-p 46; Courtesy Lokesh Chandra-pp 41, 44-45, 54-55, 56, 76-77, 78; Chokyi Palmo-pp 7, 42

ISBN 978-81-8328-475-2

Published by
Wisdom Tree
4779/23, Ansari Road
Darya Ganj, New Delhi-110 002
Ph.: 011-23247966/67/68
wisdomtreebooks@gmail.com

Printed in India

---

page 2
Nagarjuna with seven Nagas shielding him with their hoods—
hence his name. A Naga princess offers him the Prajnaparamita.

CONTENTS

FOREWORD

I welcome this small book by Mohini Kent in which she seeks to introduce the great Indian Buddhist thinker Nagarjuna to a contemporary readership. Nagarjuna is someone for whom I have immense admiration. As soon as I wake up in the morning, I recite a verse he wrote in praise of the Buddha and his explanation of emptiness.

I have the greatest respect for the world's various religious traditions, because they have evidently been immensely helpful to many people. However, by and large they depend on faith. In the Buddhist tradition, the Buddha taught us to test and verify his teaching through reason and analysis, and that is what Nagarjuna and other masters of the ancient Nalanda University have done. This scientific approach is a unique feature of the Buddhist tradition.

Nagarjuna made clear that while the teachings found in the Sanskrit Mahayana tradition are more profound than the teachings found in the Pali tradition, they do not contradict the Pali teachings. The Mahayana scriptures elaborate on themes presented and first developed in the earlier teachings of the Buddha, giving deeper and more detailed explanations of the ideas they contained. He explained that the reason we seek to understand the complex explanations of sunyata or emptiness is to understand reality and to eliminate wrong views and distorted ways of thinking. Wrong view here relates to the second of the Four Noble Truths, the origin of suffering. Once we begin to understand wisdom and eliminate wrong view, we may glimpse that achieving liberation actually is possible.

The Buddha emphasised the development of wisdom as the remedy for overcoming ignorance. And what is wisdom? It is understanding of ultimate reality, of reality as it really is. Ignorance pervades all our perceptions and in order to overcome it we cultivate an understanding of emptiness and dependent origination. Nagarjuna referred to these teachings as being like treasure. The explanation of how things arise in dependence on causes and conditions may also arouse in us a deep concern for others, which we call compassion. And compassion teaches us the value of non-harming, non-violence, which is a fitting panacea for the ills and sorrows of the world.

Indian civilisation has given rise to a long series of great thinkers and teachers endowed with both human intelligence and a sense of responsibility towards the community. The leading India nuclear physicist Raja Ramanna once told me that he had read one of Nagarjuna's texts and was amazed and proud to find an account that accords with much of what quantum physics is saying today. Similarly, ancient Indian texts are a treasure trove of knowledge about the mind and its workings. I believe they still have relevance today in the twenty-first century.

Because India and her people have, from ancient times, cherished a rich and sophisticated philosophy of non-violence at the core of their hearts, tolerance and pluralism have also flourished. These values, elaborated on by masters like Nagarjuna, continue to have great importance in the world we live in today and it is my conviction that India should take a stronger lead in presenting them to the world. I am sure many readers will join me in appreciating the author's efforts to make Nagarjuna and his ideas accessible to people today.

HH the Dalai Lama

EDITOR'S NOTE

Among the great Indian Buddhist masters, Nagarjuna is acknowledged by those who know, as one of the greatest. His explanation of sunyata, or emptiness, is a profound teaching, yet so simple and so obvious, that one wonders how we never grasped it. The sad part is that most people—across the world and across India—not only do not know about the meaning of emptiness, but have not even heard of Nagarjuna. Yet emptiness was only one of the ways that Nagarjuna enriched people's lives with his profound understanding of the paths the Buddha opened for us. Long, long forgotten, those paths are beginning to open again in this new era, and the great masters who grasped and spread the message are only now beginning to emerge from the past into the present.

When I dreamt of a series of books on the masters of Buddhism in India, to introduce readers to some of the greatest Indians who ever lived, Nagarjuna was an obvious choice. But to find the right author who would present this profound thinker in a way that would reach and interest people who are only now beginning to discover the immense profundity and yet essential simplicity of Buddhism, was not an easy task. There are many scholars who have the knowledge and the understanding of his teachings, but very few who could communicate this to those just beginning to rediscover a philosophy taught so many centuries ago.

At a teaching by His Holiness the Dalai Lama, I started telling Mohini Kent—whom I have known for very many years as a writer, a thinker, a dreamer and a doer—about my idea of a series of simple, readable books about the early masters of Buddhism forgotten in the country of their birth. I realised that Mohini Kent would be an ideal author. She was utterly taken aback. But very quickly said 'yes' she would like to do it but it would require a lot of time and research because, as she says in her introduction to the book, she is not a scholar herself. But once she decides to take on something, I know she does it with total commitment.

The result is this very thoughtful and thought-provoking book, presented in a manner that even the uninitiated will find very readable and yet one that leaves you enriched and awakened.

It did that for me, and I am sure it will do that for you.

I am deeply and eternally grateful to Dr Lokesh Chandra for his illuminating insights and the patience with which he bore with my questions and eagerness to learn over the past several years, and for his help in practical terms, with photographs and clarifications, for this hopefully ongoing series of books. Chokyi Palmo was very generous with giving some of her photographs for the books and Achal Kumar generously gave of his time and expertise in taking some expert quality photographs; Kshipra Simon was always ready when needed to take more photographs. Choyang-la, Ashok Wangdi, Bryan Mulvihill, Dipnkar Khanna—all helped in a variety of ways to make this dream a reality.

Aruna Vasudev
Series Editor

INTRODUCTION

Someone who has acted carelessly, but later becomes careful and attentive,
is as beautiful as the bright moon emerging from the clouds.

—Nagarjuna

The twenty-first century is unique in the annals of human history, both for its opportunities and its challenges. We, who live in this century, are unique human beings, poised as we are on the cusp of nature's next evolutionary thrust forward. Each one of us can participate in the great adventure of consciousness without being dogged by dogma or circumscribed by rigid religious and social rules. Personal freedom, for many, is theirs for the asking. The future, it seems, is in our hands. By personal effort, we can invent ourselves and shape our lives.

This is also the message of Nagarjuna, the ancient Buddhist monk. Legends revolve around his birth and death, as is customary with great heroes. Who he was, where he lived, or even when he lived, is all a bit of a mystery, but there is nothing shadowy about the message he left behind. According to traditional accounts, he was a scholar-monk at Nalanda University, the great Indian centre of Buddhist learning, in the late second century AD. He went on to become the head at Nalanda, his

left

Nagarjuna seated on a lotus with Nagas protecting his head. At his feet lie his alms bowl, golden *bumpa* (ritual vessel) and coral in a vase on a lotus leaf. In the water are corals shaped like Dharmachakras, and various fruits. Volumes of the Prajnaparamita are stacked on his right.

mental prowess being such that he alone would defeat scores of scholars in debate. His philosophy and writings fundamentally influenced Buddhism in the millennia to follow. Nagarjuna's most famous work—the *Mulamadhyamakakarika* (*Fundamental Verses of the Middle Way*)—introduced the concept of emptiness, and after Gautama Buddha, Nagarjuna remains the single most important figure in Buddhist thought. In fact, in the Mahayana traditions, his work has earned him the sobriquet of 'The Second Buddha'.

Frankly, much of the *Madhyamaka* text is baffling, maddeningly so to lay readers. It can seem like an exceptionally difficult mental maze from which it is impossible to find one's way out! However, the one thing that stands out clearly is its emphasis on reason. Reason itself helps in deconstructing reason, to assimilate all knowledge that transcends reason. And that is why the *Madhyamaka* is important for our present age.

This book is not for the scholar, nor do I claim to be a Buddhist scholar. This book is for the simple seeker who, like me, is trying to understand. The concept of emptiness is truly difficult to put across in simple words, i.e. the notion that people and things, all phenomena in fact, lack a fixed, immutable essence. Had that not been the case, it would be impossible to be transformed into something else. It is because of interdependence and lack of rigid, immutable personal essence of being that we can change, that samsara (the world of suffering) can flow into nirvana (enlightenment), which is why the Buddha too was transformed. It is a frightening concept because people do not like change. They feel safe and secure in sticking to the familiar. What's more, each one of us likes to believe that we have our own independent thoughts and ideas, and we are not comfortable being told that there is nothing definitive in us that cannot be changed.

The famous Vietnamese monk, Thich Nhat Hanh, explains the Madhyamaka concept of emptiness and interdependence as there being no first or ultimate cause for anything that occurs. Instead, all things are dependent on innumerable causes and conditions that are themselves dependent on other innumerable causes and conditions. So there is no independent, inherent existence of any phenomenon, including the self. Nagarjuna sets up a formula of four possibilities, each one of which he then rejects: Something is, it is not, it both is and is not, and it neither is nor is not. What Nagarjuna really refuted were modes of thought, opinions, views, statements and so on. He took the middle path between clinging to either being or non-being. This tendency to cling to concepts is the root of suffering. His Middle Way is to see things as they truly are, and to try and understand that nothing in the world actually exists in absolute terms, just as nothing perishes completely.

This interdependence also forms a fundamental basis for the Mahayana teachings on compassion and ethics, and the emphasis on ethical living extends to environmental ethics as well.

The interdependence of all phenomena, persons, feelings, and everything else, including the flow of samsara into nirvana, is a message of great hope. Suffering is just an interim process, and as we travel along the continuum, we will attain nirvana. The nature of samsara and nirvana are not really different because the former is capable of being transformed into the latter. As our self-knowledge grows, our sufferings will diminish. It seems that as long as we are in the world, we cannot avoid suffering, but we suffer and are stressed because of our ignorance. The world will exist as long as it is driven by desire. If desire is the cause of the world remaining in motion, and desire leads to suffering, then elimination of desire can eliminate suffering. The remedy is to increase our true knowledge by transcending the chattering mind, and thus, Nagarjuna gave us the concept of the Silent Mind.

Nagarjuna's message is one of great personal empowerment and it gains more urgency in our present century because traditional religious societies have broken down, the old certainties have vanished and people are lonely, lost and confused. We struggle with ourselves, with our relationships and with the world around us. It is not easy to have an individual moral compass in this bewildering age.

The real karmic task of the twenty-first century is to reconcile spirit and matter.

In traditional religious societies, life had two dimensions—one that involved other people and another that focused on the inner dimension. An outer life and an inner life. Subjective feelings such as jealousy, pettiness, greed and other ugly thoughts were examined and weeded out as much as possible, and this helped shape character. In modern society, however, the first dimension has almost completely taken over and worldly success is what counts. The modality is only social. The second dimension has disappeared. People are no longer interested in deeper motives. No one asks, *have you crafted a beautiful soul?*

Even an eminent scientist such as Albert Einstein said, 'Try not to become a man of success, rather try to become a man of value.'

Dharma, or the principle of duty, morality and righteousness, depends upon time, circumstances, age and the community to which one belongs. Dharma, in Hinduism, mainly refers to one's duty done according to the law of one's own being, but there are many interpretations of dharma. Each one of us has a unique dharma because no two people are identical. In Buddhism, dharma or dhamma means the eternal truth, the truth of the universe, the truth contained in scriptures and the cosmic law and order. For practicing Buddhists, it means the teachings of the Buddha, known as Buddha-Dharma. Unlike in other world religions, the Buddha refused to discuss metaphysical questions. Religion means the belief in a personal god or gods, belief in a controlling power and reverence for a supernatural power regarded as the governor of the universe, so in that sense, Buddhism barely qualifies. Religions have sacred histories, symbols and narratives to explain the meaning of life, its origins, cosmic laws and human nature as well as religious and moral laws to govern society. The Buddha preferred that the human being concentrate on transforming himself. The Buddha said that debating whether the world had a beginning or an end, or what happens after death, is the equivalent of being hit by an arrow but refusing medical treatment until one has learnt about the specific wood from which the arrow was made, who fired it and why. Instead, the Buddha approached life pragmatically. He compared his dharma to a raft that can carry the soul across the ocean of life and death, but which should be treated as a mere instrument (of enlightenment) and not clung to after it has served its purpose. Rather, it should be abandoned instead of being carried about. Nagarjuna's teachings are firmly rooted in the original teachings of the Buddha, i.e. in the Buddha-Dharma. It is a definite code of conduct in the world, with morality and ethics at its core. It brings with it a totally different concept of one's individual relationship with the cosmos because it places full responsibility on the human being for his actions and the outcomes of those actions. The ineluctable law of karma holds that the quality of our current and future lives is dependent upon the quality of our personal behaviour, both now and in our previous lives. Buddhism gives us the guidelines to help manifest spirit in matter, in ourselves, by individual transformation. It is a truly rational religion that does not require blind faith and beliefs. At its heart are ethics, not only theology and metaphysics. It is eminently suited to the twenty-first century where man's rational mind is highly developed and the levels of education are high.

The law of karma, or the law of action, is a wonderful thing. Every action has a reaction and the universe holds up a mirror to us. It returns the energy you send out to it. The Buddha's path makes clear that ethical conduct is based on right thought, right speech, right action and right livelihood. Moral instructions are an integral part of Buddhist tradition and scriptures. The Buddha provided the basic guidelines in the Eightfold Path and non-injury or non-violence towards all living beings, from humans to the smallest insect, creates a kind relationship with all beings. The Five Precepts of no killing, no stealing, no lying, no sexual misconduct and no intoxicants are the bedrock of a Buddhist's beliefs. Lay persons are encouraged to voluntarily practise them for they lead to refinement of the consciousness. In Nagarjuna's work, the matter of ethics is clearly discussed in his *Ratnavali* or *Precious Garland of Letters to the King*.

Life is a journey of consciousness, of becoming more aware, and it is not a task to be relegated to old age or to be used as a prop in adversity. Instead, it is the very staff of life, to be grasped at every moment to allow us to walk more easily, breathe more freely. We must do it just when it seems almost impossible, for example, in a metro tube train during rush hour, or while walking in a crowded park. We can walk consciously, as a seeker would, instead of living haphazardly, our energy depleted by wayward emotions. We must try to gather our scattered consciousness and work on ourselves every minute.

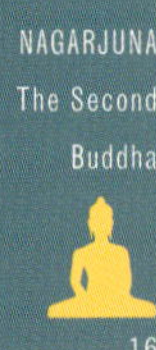

There is a gulf between what we are at present and what we can become. How do we overcome that? By the Buddhist practice of sincere mindfulness. How do we overcome suffering? By silencing our minds, by eschewing phantom desires, by identifying with the real instead of the unreal. That is Nagarjuna's promise to us. Personal effort is the key.

Our mistake is in judging the future by our present possibilities, for we must exceed our present limitations. It is within our grasp…but first, we must do our homework.

Mohini Kent

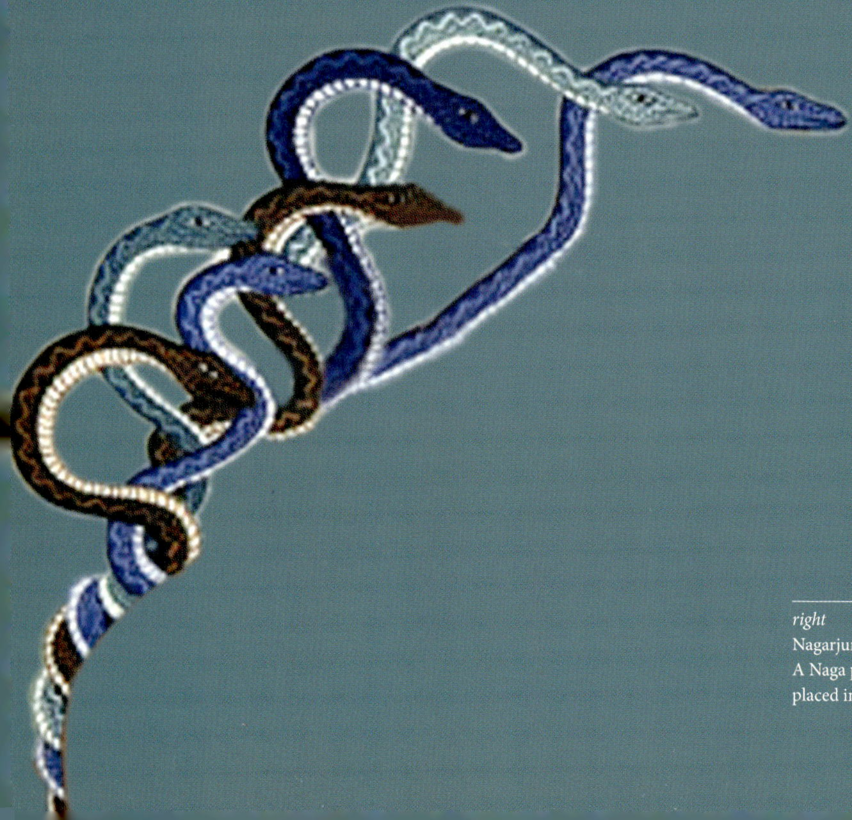

right
Nagarjuna seated beneath a rhododendron tree on a floating platform. A Naga princess offers him the Prajnaparamita. Its twelve volumes are placed in a bookrack on his left.

Shakyamuni Buddha with pandits of
Nalanda University. Nagarjuna studied
at the university and went on to become
its Head.

NAGARJUNA
LEGENDS
AND
MESSAGE

If the present and the future depend on the past, then the present and the future would have existed in the past. If the present and future did not exist there, how could the present and the future be dependent on it?

—Nagarjuna

Nagarjuna was the founder of Madhyamaka Buddhism who transformed the understanding of Buddhist traditions for future millennia, but the man remains an enigma. Nagarjuna's visionary interpretation of the concept of the emptiness of all things and his substantial body of Buddhist works earned him the sobriquet of 'The Second Buddha' in the Mahayana tradition, but precious little is known about his actual life. Scholars are unable to agree on a timeline for his life (in the first three centuries AD) or a place (almost anywhere in India) or even the number of Nagarjunas that history has seen (ranging from one to four). His career has been located varyingly throughout India—often in the South (Satavahana stronghold) or further North (in Daksinakosala), but also sometimes in the West, Northwest or Northeast. Most of the extant accounts of his life were written long after his death. The two most extensive biographies of him (one in Chinese and another in Tibetan)

left
Nagarjuna in the Dharmachakra mudra with Manjushri in the clouds on the right, above.

were written several centuries after his death, by which time his reputation was so magnified that these accounts incorporate much lively material, some of which attains mythic proportions. Claims about his life are often asserted as if they are facts known to be absolutely true, which they are not at all. Thorough research does suggest that none of the commonly advanced arguments about the time period or place of his life can be proved, that it could have been later Nagarjunas who became the authors of pseudepigrapha.

They say his birth was predicted in various sutras, such as The Descent into Lanka Sutra, the Lankavatara Sutra, that contains the prophecy of the Buddha that—'in Vedali, in the Southern region, there will be an illustrious monk of great renown, bearing the appellation Naga (or by the name Nagahvaya). He will destroy the views of existence and non-existence.' The most important doctrine of the Lankavatara Sutra is the teaching of consciousness as the only reality. In it, the Buddha asserts that all the objects of the world and the names and forms of experience are merely manifestations of the mind. The question is whether the prophecy really referred to Nagarjuna or not. Vedali presumably refers to the Vidarbha region bordering the Andhra region where Nagarjuna was born. It also contained the provisional name of 'Naga' but Nagarjuna apparently had a student named Nagahvaya. However, the reference to 'destroying the views of existence and non-existence' also seems to point to Nagarjuna.

According to the majority of Tibetan sources, an astrologer had predicted his premature death. In order to avert the cruel fate, his parents decided to have him ordained as a Buddhist monk. It seems that he escaped an early death, being under the protection of his teacher, Rahulabdara, carrying out various practices under his guidance.

An alternative version has it that there was a predication at his birth that he would live only for seven days but that this period could be stretched to seven years, provided his parents made offerings to one hundred monks. His parents must have obliged because seven days passed without mishap, but before he could reach the next milestone of seven years, his parents had sent Nagarjuna off to the Nalanda

Monastic University in North India. There he met the Buddhist master, Saraha, who encouraged him to become a renunciate and recite the Amitabha mantra for a long life. Nagarjuna followed his counsel, joined the monastery and was 'born again' under the name 'Shrimanta'.

There are no actual biographical sources solely for Nagarjuna; instead, we need to look at different texts to glean as much information as possible. There are Indian texts; some of the Sanskrit ones, that had been translated into Tibetan and Chinese, no longer exist. As the Tibetans say, if we have two people who agree, then we have two fools!

The other story about Nagarjuna's life comes from the Chinese text *Gaosengchuan*, written by Kumarajiva, a brilliant Buddhist monk from Kuchea, a kingdom located on the branch of the Silk Road that ran along the northern edge of the Taklamakan Desert and which became an important Buddhist centre. Kumarajiva was the son of an Indian Brahmin and a Kuchean princess. His mother became a Buddhist nun when he was seven-years old and he grew up studying the Buddhist doctrine with eminent scholars. He could memorise 36,000 words a day. He was ordained as a monk when he was twenty and he died at the age of either seventy or hundred, around the year 409 AD. Kumarajiva revolutionised Chinese Buddhism by translating more than 300 volumes of Buddhist scriptures from Sanskrit into Chinese languages, working with about 800 scholars. His most important work was the translation of Nagarjuna's texts of the Madhyamaka school, which became the basic texts of the Chinese 'Three Treatise' school of Buddhism. Kumarajiva became an adherent of the Madhyamaka doctrine, the treatise of the Middle Way. He was so brilliant that Emperor Yao Hsing wanted him to break his vow of chastity in order to pass on his genes to children who would be as clever as him. So he compelled him to move into a palace with ten 'singing girls'. Although the monk accepted the palace and the women, it is said he retained his purity and was faithful to his Buddhist principles. It is said when he was about to die he declared that if he had made no mistakes in the translations of the sutras, then his tongue would not burn when he was cremated. If, however, he had made mistakes, and the Buddha was not pleased, then his tongue would be cremated with him. And his tongue did not burn when he was cremated.

Kumarajiva writes that Nagarjuna's epiphany came about because of a traumatic event. He and his friends practised psychokinesis (*rddhi*s) that gave them the power to render themselves invisible. Using that power, they entered the king's harem to pleasure themselves by seducing the royal ladies. The plan, however, went awry when they were caught red-handed by the palace guards. At that crucial moment, the power failed his two friends, who were apprehended and executed. Nagarjuna, however, successfully turned invisible again and escaped. Shaken to the core by the experience, Nagarjuna was instantly reformed. He realised that the gratification of sensual cravings is a potent cause of suffering, i.e. he realised the Second Noble Truth of Buddhism.

The First Noble Truth is that there is suffering and the world is impermanent. Suffering is the evitable outcome when we cling to impermanent phenomena as though they were permanent. Madhyamaka philosophy expresses the truth that all things are empty of inherent existence or substance, hence they are all relative and transitory.

The Second Noble Truth is that there is a cause of suffering. The suffering is due to our mental misconceptions and our mental and emotional clinging to relative phenomena as though they are absolute reality. The root cause of suffering arises out of our confusing the unreal with the real. Ignorance of the true nature of all phenomena, i.e. their lack of inherent substance or their sunyata (emptiness) leads to our anguish and misery.

The Third Noble Truth is that there is an end to suffering. Suffering is not permanent or everlasting because that too is relative and conditioned. And because emptiness too is empty, because relativity and the conditioned state themselves are not absolute, suffering is not ultimate. While the mundane nature of the conditioned is 'conditionedness', in its ultimate nature, the conditioned is itself the undivided, unconditioned reality. The ultimate reality is beyond the distinctions that hold in the world of the determinate, yet the ultimate reality is not wholly separate from the determinate but is the real nature of the determinate itself. It is because we are already identical to the unconditioned reality that we can recognise this truth and become liberated from the imagination that we are not, and thereby end our suffering.

The Fourth Noble Truth is that there is a path that leads to the end of suffering. The Middle Way is the non-exclusive way that destroys the ignorance of clinging to the relative as absolute. Through the method of criticism, extreme views are shown to lead to contradictions which reveal the truth of sunyata with regard to all things. Ultimately, even sunyata or relativity itself is denied as absolute, revealing the unutterable unconditioned reality which is the ultimate nature of ourselves and all things.

His Life

There are constant contradictions about Nagarjuna's lifespan but the second century AD seems to be widely accepted as the broad period, with the years of his life placed around 150–250 AD. This seems to tally with the life of his foremost disciple, Aryadeva, who was the author of the treatise *Four Hundred Verses* on the actions of a Bodhisattva's yoga. Nagarjuna, together with Aryadeva, is credited with founding the Madhyamaka School of Mahayana Buddhism. But if we look for secure facts, we are likely to meet constant contradictions and be left feeling frustrated. It is often stated in scholarly references that Nagarjuna lived in the second century AD, sometimes with the latter half of it specified. While the general consensus is that Nagarjuna lived to around the age of one hundred, some scholars have claimed that it is neither impossible nor absurd to ascribe Nagarjuna's age as around 200 years, which would cover a period ranging from the first century BC to the early second century AD.

It seems he was born into a Hindu Brahmin family in South India in the Vidarbha kingdom, in contemporary Maharashtra state. He seems to have lived during the reign of Gautamiputra Satakarni, a historical king of the northern Satavahana dynasty, who ruled for thirty years, from 166–196 AD. Archaeological evidence points at Amravati; the Satavahanas were patrons of the stupas in Amravati where the Buddha taught the Kalachakra Tantra. Nagarjuna's *Suhrlekha* (*Letter to a Good Friend*) and *Ratnavali* (*Precious Garland*) seem to be addressed to the king, advising him to adopt Buddhist ways to bring peace and pacifism to the land. The king appears to have taken no notice of his advice, having engaged in constant battles against the northern Shaka Satrap rulers in unsuccessful attempts to expand his empire, but the imperial correspondence seems to place those years of Nagarjuna's life between 150 and 200 AD. This also means that Tibetan sources that place his emigration from the Andhra region to Nalanda University, in present-day Bihar, are basically accurate. Nagarjuna eventually became the abbot of Nalanda and his scholarship was such that he, alone, defeated 500 non-Buddhist monks in debate. He also expelled 8000 monks who had not adhered to the *vinaya* monastic rules of discipline.

Nalanda was the site of the greatest Buddhist monastery of scholastic excellence in India. In the invigorating intellectual environment of North Indian scholastic institutions of the time, Nagarjuna became an outstanding philosopher. He studied the tantra and sutras, with Ratnamati and Saraha, and all other traditional branches of learning. But he also studied alchemy from a Brahmin. It is said he acquired the knowledge of how to transmute iron into gold, or the secret of the philosopher's stone. The legendary alchemical substance is also believed to be the elixir of life, potentially leading to immortality. It is said that Nagarjuna lived for hundreds of years and then had to choose voluntary death. Meanwhile, his alchemical skills also meant that Nagarjuna knew the secret of producing food and so was able to feed all the Nalanda monks during a time of famine.

Other Legends

Even his name 'Nagarjuna' is the stuff of legends. His mastery of magic and meditation had earned him a place at the Naga king's table at the bottom of the sea. Patalatala, the watery kingdom of the Nagas (snakes who were water deities), was a fearful place to visit unless, like Nagarjuna, you were invited. His fame had spread even to that realm, and one day, two youths appeared at Nalanda. Their natural scent of sandalwood gave them away to the philosopher, who correctly surmised that they were sons of the Naga king, Nagaraja, sent on an errand in human form. Cobras are traditionally found in sandalwood groves. The lads confessed as to who they really were. Whatever their errand, Nagarjuna took advantage of their visit to press them for the best sandalwood to carve eight statues of the goddess Tara, as well as to enlist their help in constructing relevant temples. They left after

right
Manjushri on a lion is the presiding deity of Nagarjuna. Crossing the ocean of existence, the devotee attains the pure land of Manjushri.

promising to ask their father and returned to the ocean. The Naga king agreed to the request, on the condition that Nagarjuna would visit his underwater kingdom to teach them.

Nagarjuna had another reason for engaging with the Naga king. Legend has it that the sea serpents guarded the Prajnaparamita, or Perfection of Wisdom Sutra, one version of which the Buddha had entrusted to them for safekeeping. When the Enlightened One had taught the far-reaching discriminating awareness of the Prajnaparamita, he handed one version to the gods, one to the Yaksha lords of wealth (nature spirits, usually benevolent, who are caretakers of natural treasures), and another one to the Nagas.

Nagarjuna, through the great merit he had earned, fulfilled the superhuman task of living on the ocean bed to teach the Nagas. He made them many offerings and satisfied them on every score. Pleased, the Naga king presented him with the Hundred Thousand Verse, the Prajnaparamita Sutra. All the verses that is, except the last two, which the Naga king withheld so that Nagarjuna would have to return to teach them further. However, Nagarjuna was also given valuable Naga clay with which he built many temples and stupas.

His feat also earned the scholar the appellation of Nagarjuna, meaning the noble serpent. It is an amalgamation of Naga and Arjuna, the great warrior of the Mahabharata epic. Arjuna was a celebrated archer and Nagarjuna's arrows of Dharma teachings also invariably found their mark.

Once back from the land of the Nagas, Nagarjuna wrote his commentary on the Prajnaparamita. The problem of the two missing verses of The Hundred Thousand Verse Perfection of Wisdom Sutra was solved by transposing the last two chapters of The Eight Thousand Verse, Prajnaparamita Sutra, into the former. Later, in Tibet, these teachings formed part of the philosophy of Tibetan Buddhism.

Once, when Nagarjuna was teaching the sutra on land, six cobras came and shielded him from the sun by joining their hoods over his head. The iconic image of Nagarjuna depicts him with cobras forming an umbrella over his head with their hoods. A king cobra rising up behind Nagarjuna is reminiscent of a story of the Buddha, where he was once deep in meditation and it began to rain, when a king cobra arose behind him and shielded him from the elements with its hood. All snakes and fish are symbolic of the Nagas. Nagarjuna is depicted with a vase to his right for holding his monk's possessions, meaning that he kept his monastic vows. Dressed in the robes of a fully ordained monk, he is depicted seated in the Bodhisattva posture, denoting his friendship and concern for all sentient beings.

Banabhatta is a seventh-century Sanskrit writer and author of the *Harsacarita*, the biography of the Buddhist Indian Emperor Harsha, which is the first Sanskrit text to make the connection between Nagarjuna and the king Satavahana.

In the *Harsacarita* (Deeds of Emperor Harsha), Banabhatta wrote: 'Eventually, a monk called Nagarjuna was brought to Patalatala by the Nagas, begged this string from the Lord of the Nagas and received it.' Upon returning to the human world, Nagarjuna gave it to his friend, King Satavahana, Lord of the Three Oceans. Thus, in time, the texts were passed down through disciples to scholars such as Banabhatta.

His Message

While Nagarjuna is particularly associated with the Prajnaparamita Sutra, he is truly famous for his writings on emptiness. His legendary work is the *Madhyamaka Shastra* (Treatise on the Middle Way), also known as *Mulamadhyamakakarika* (Fundamental Verses on the Middle Way). His theme is the Bodhisattva's path to buddhahood. Enlightenment may be achieved by acquiring merit and the perfection of wisdom, meaning knowledge of emptiness. Within the Tibetan tradition especially, Nagarjuna is viewed as the second Buddha.

By the time Nagarjuna had matured as a philosopher, the concept of 'zero' had shaken up all existing metaphysical systems of philosophy. Since the third century BC, the concept of zero had been helping to redefine the world. Nagarjuna took the new concept of emptiness, the void, and changed Buddhism. What it meant was that all phenomena lack inherently stable existence, i.e. they are empty

and exist only because of interdependence. It is because of this interdependence that one can hope to be transformed. If each phenomenon was fixed in its essence, then it would not be possible for change and transformation into something else to take place. The Tathagata Buddha (the One Who Came and Went) was transformed only because of this nature of interdependence and emptiness of all phenomena. It signified the hope of change and enlightenment for all. Nagarjuna said that whatever phenomenon arises is empty of eternal essence, and to recognise it as such is the middle path. To realise it, we have to be conscious of how we live, of what we do, of how we interact with each other and with the earth; in short, mindful living.

Nagarjuna gave hope to our perennial quest to understand the world and ourselves. So far, all phenomena had been viewed as being fixed and their inherent substance as stable and unchanging. Good was good and bad was bad; the turbulent suffering of ignorant material life was the opposite of the enlightened spiritual existence and the wheel of samsara, of anguish and pain, was the opposite of the bliss of nirvana. He showed us that change and transformation, including enlightenment, is possible because of interdependence. Phenomena are open to change precisely because they lack inherent fixed nature and are, therefore, empty. The very nature of our existence and all the phenomena around us is emptiness and interdependence, which is why the Buddha too was transformed.

His analysis deconstructed the world to show that nothing is incontrovertible, nothing has immutable essence. Instead, everything flows into each other and existence is interdependence. The kernel of bliss already exists in suffering. Material deprivation can lead to spiritual treasure. Conflict can blossom into friendship. Samsara can flow into nirvana. All conceivable change is indeed our nature and that's where we enter the realm of freedom of individual choice. In fact, it is up to us. Things can go either way, so the direction in which they go can be shaped by our deeds. Realisation depends on what we do and how we exist within the world. The law of karma is operated by us. He showed that Buddhism does not belong merely inside the covers of sacred texts or within the robes of

left
Aryadeva and Nagarjuna—with Manushri on a lion in the clouds.

monks and monasteries but on the street and in the minutiae of our daily lives. It is one of the most empowering messages the world has ever heard. The Buddhist must constantly reform himself and transform the world around him. That is the true mission of Buddhism.

We could be transformed if we move purposefully on that path. First, however, we must understand our own nature. The Buddha, Siddhartha Gautama Shakyamuni, had already signalled that he preferred us to spend our valuable time, rationed by life, on self-mastery instead of pondering on ultimate knowledge. He pointedly refused to respond to metaphysical questions about the existence of God and the beginning or end of the world. Instead, he placed emphasis on directing our energy to understanding and curing mental ills, destructive psychological tendencies and attachments. When a human being is kept constantly on the boil by emotions, where is the need to seek an answer to the end of the world? Until and unless human beings introspect and develop a state of meditative enlightenment, they will be trapped in ignorance and suffering. Knowledge can alleviate suffering, but one has to work for that. The Buddha provided the Four Error (*Catuskoti*) denial method to discourage futile metaphysical meanderings. His response to the question about the beginning of the world was to say: i) the world does not have a beginning ii) it does not *not* have a beginning iii) It does not have and not have a beginning iv) nor does it neither have nor not have a beginning. In effect, he said nothing, neither confirming nor denying the proposition. He recommended to his followers to take no position whatsoever.

The Middle Way is the path between the extremes of sensual pleasure and asceticism. Enlightenment is the state beyond the agitated, dissatisfied mind. It is a state of freedom. What it means is that we can actually take charge of our own lives, instead of being controlled by the environment. At present, most of us, most of the time, live in a state of reaction. Our time and our energies are absorbed by reaction, not action.

Nagarjuna talked precisely about the lack of autonomous existence of phenomena. Everything depends upon everything else, which in turn depends upon other phenomena. It means that our lives unfold in the context of nature and society. Within that context, we are free to choose our attitudes

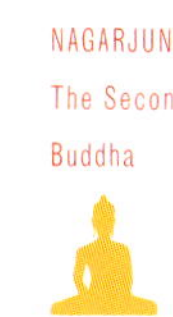

and deeds, our karma, accumulating meritorious karma or harmful and negative karma. Thus, our fate is in our hands, and so we can transform ourselves. The nature of buddhahood is given to all, but realisation depends upon our efforts. The Buddhist vow to avoid suffering is not an ascetic shrinking from the world but a pledge to seek out the nirvana that already exists within this world. Suffering and peace, both are possibilities that lie before us, and the outcome depends on our actions and interaction. Merit and wisdom can lead to enlightenment.

This is an immensely liberating message, even for the twenty-first century. Everyone is engaged in the quest for happiness and if we reach beyond our conditioned minds, moulded by our circumstances, we can attain the silence within which the true reality is revealed to us.

Our individual mind is a mega-computer, working incessantly to process the fresh data received from the world. By analysing, judging, comparing, rejecting, accepting, scheming and endlessly weighing pros and cons and arguing with ourselves, in effect, we're creating our own subjective reality, our own fictional world to dwell in. The inner chatter never dies, and in our contemporary world, minds are stimulated as never before.

The Buddha preached the Middle Way in his first sermon, i.e. the path between the extremes of self-indulgence and self-mortification. Nagarjuna went a step further by recognising a middle path between permanence and annihilation. By his day, Buddhists had accepted the concept of *svabhava* or intrinsic essence of a person, natural phenomena and the karmic process of evolution. They argued that without a fixed *svabhava* of each, there would be no reckoning of the karmic process. If there was not an essential nature in each one that had to be transformed, then Buddhist practices would not effect any real change.

Nagarjuna argued that change was only possible if people did not have fixed *svabhava*. He distinguished ways in which things could be causally brought about. In his famed argument, he said that phenomena could be produced: i) from themselves ii) from other things iii) from both themselves and from other things iv) from neither.

Neither from itself nor from another,

Nor from both,

Nor without a cause,

Does anything whatever, anywhere arise.

He argued that if anything has an intrinsic nature or fixed *svabhava*, then how can it change? Such a change would destroy the original premise by destroying its essential *svabhava*, so that is not logical. We do not experience empirically that which does not change, but only experience it through the filter of ourselves. Nagarjuna used the Buddha's own Four Error method to create fresh insight into the nature of reality. To believe that all beings have intrinsic *svabhava* means to acknowledge the permanence of all things. On the other hand, it's an equally mistaken belief to think that nothing exists, i.e. to believe in annihilation. For Nagarjuna, the true nature of reality is not non-existence but the absence of immutable existence in each phenomenon. All persons, phenomena and even concepts lack fixed *svabhava*; hence, they are responsive to change and transformation. Change is the only essence of existence. Babies are born, they mature, age and die. Suffering can be changed into enlightenment. All this is possible only if entities are empty (*sunya*) of unalterable essence and capable of transformation.

Sunyata, or voidness, is what constitutes ultimate reality in Buddhism. It is not a negation of existence but rather the undifferentiated, non-dualistic core out of which arises all forms, phenomena and dualities. Sunyata could also be interpreted as the lack of inherent existence of self after the physical and mental sheaths of existence have been shed. In ancient Indian thought, the five sheaths, or bodies, of existence are the physical, the nervous envelope, the mental sheath, the body of knowledge and the body of bliss. Nagarjuna's *Madhyamaka* is also sometimes called the *Sunyavada*, the doctrine of voidness.

Nagarjuna's fundamental theme is transformation of the Bodhisattva through the acquisition of

right
Nagarjuna surrounded by mahasiddhas.

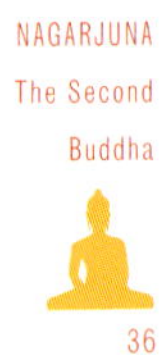

sufficient merit and wisdom on the path to enlightenment, buddhahood. All logic, all philosophies, must be discarded after they have served their purpose, leaving behind only non-dualistic wisdom and compassion.

The ultimate goal of life in Buddhism, as in Hinduism and Jainism, is the attainment of nirvana (or moksha in Hinduism) through the extinguishing of all desires and karmas. It is desire, and the inherited karma it creates, that propels us ever forward into reincarnation, in order to balance it all out. The pacification of the mind by extinguishing desire and annulling all karma would lead to reduced suffering in the world, and ultimately, the prevention of rebirth. The unique contribution of Buddhism is the concept of 'no self' or 'no soul' (*anatman*). What this means is that everything from one's personal identity to external objects can be analysed down to their atomic components. Thus, shedding all desire and karma, one evolves into *sunya*, the void, leaving no part to live on as the spiritual entity, the atman.

However, if all extant phenomena are in a constant state of flux, then what is the difference between the saint and the sinner, between the enlightened Buddha and unenlightened beings?

Nagarjuna had received his philosophical training in the traditional Buddhist texts and through intense debates. He criticised all theoretical justification for portraying sharp distinctions between samsara, the world of pain and suffering, and nirvana, the state of absolute peace, silence and freedom. He did not portray the historical Buddha as the pure embodiment of peace, as quite distinct from the tumultuous suffering of the world. Instead, no demarcation exists between the pained world and the disciplined spiritual practices that lead to enlightenment. All human beings can, in theory, travel along the continuum to enlightenment. Both samsara and nirvana are given to us, and it's up to us to avoid suffering by realising the potentiality of nirvana by our own efforts. The Buddha was transformed only because of interdependence.

Nagarjuna is in the Middle Path between permanence and nihilism, between 'it is' and 'it is not'. The wise do not take a fixed position by saying that it exists or that it does not exist.

If there is not an essential immutable nature in each phenomena, then what is it that will have been transformed? However, if such an essential fixed nature does exist, then what *can* be transformed?

Unexpected support came from the scientific advances made in the twentieth century by Einstein, Niels Bohr, Robert Oppenheimer and others studying the realm of atomic and subatomic particles. In his book *The Tao of Physics*, Fritjof Capra writes: 'Quantum theory thus reveals a basic oneness of the universe. It shows that we cannot decompose the world into independently existing smallest units. As we penetrate into matter, nature does not show us any isolated "building blocks", but rather appears as a complicated web of relations between the various parts of the whole. These relations always include the observer in an essential way. The human observers constitute the final link in the chain of observational processes, and the properties of any atomic object can be understood only in terms of the object's interaction with the observer.'

The boundaries of suffering and enlightenment overlap and the Buddha's example makes us aware of the possibilities of life. There is no limit to human consciousness but it has to be developed, at first through the mind, then by moving beyond the mind. The mind is a helper to begin with and helps us to understand. Later, the mind becomes a hindrance, when the arrogance of knowledge leads to ruin. The ultimate truth has to be approached by using the staff of knowledge; nirvana is not a process to be reasoned out, but one to be attained.

Fritjof Capra also wrote in *The Turning Point*: 'Scientists, therefore, are responsible for their research, not only intellectually but also morally. This responsibility has become an important issue in many of today's sciences, but especially so in physics, in which the results of quantum mechanics and relativity theory have opened up two very different paths for physicists to pursue. They may lead us—to put it in extreme terms—to the Buddha or to the Bomb, and it is up to each of us to decide which path to take.'

We have to make choices. Only by making choices through living and acting consciously and mindfully, minute by minute in body, mind and speech can we progress.

Desires cease with thought. Truth is both absolute and relative, because in the absolute sense, there are no 'things' but in the relative sense, all concrete objects exist. Everything is actual or not actual. Or neither actual nor not actual, according to the Buddha's teachings. Thus, there are two truths. The absolute truth is devoid of mental constructions.

The Buddha is quoted as having alluded to himself as the 'Tathagata' instead of 'I'. The word is generally interpreted to mean 'one who has thus gone' or 'one who has thus come', i.e. one who is beyond all coming and going, beyond all transitory phenomena. One who has transcended the cycle of suffering in the samsara and rebirth. It implies one who has transcended the human condition. The nature of the Tathagata is the nature of the world, which means that we too can be transformed, as the Buddha was.

When all dharmas are empty, what is endless? What has an end?
What is endless and with an end? What is not endless and not with an end?
What is it? What is other? What is permanent? What is impermanent?
What is impermanent and permanent? What is neither?
There is no dharma whatsoever taught by the Buddha to whomever, whenever, wherever.

—Mulamadhyamakakarika

Legends of His Death

It is not known for how long Nagarjuna lived or when he died. The legends surrounding his death, like those of his birth, seem to reflect his stature in the Buddhist traditions. The general consensus is that he lived for 100 years, but some scholars claimed that his life spanned 200 years. Yet others claim that he lived for 600 years.

According to the *Kathasaritsagar*, an eleventh-century Sanskrit collection of morality tales and fairy stories compiled by the Brahmin Somadeva, one Nagarjuna was the minister of King Udayibhadra. However, almost a millennium had lapsed between the life and times of Nagarjuna and Somadeva, so the text has little historical value; yet, it has an interesting tale to tell.

right
Nagarjuna with his hands in the Dharmachakra mudra—gesture of teaching of the wheel of Dharma.

King Udayibhadra had a son, the crown prince Kumara Shaktiman, who was in a hurry to ascend the throne. His mother pointed out that the king's life was inextricably linked with Nagarjuna's life and advised him to ask the minister for his head. As a being of compassion, Nagarjuna could not refuse. As anticipated, Nagarjuna agreed to the prince's request to die, but how would it be done? Kumara Shaktiman could not decapitate him with a sword. Nagarjuna told the prince that he could only die if his head was cut off with a blade of *kusha* grass. That was the karmic residue of a previous life where Nagarjuna had killed an ant while he was cutting grass. Kumara Shaktiman struck off his head with the recommended blade of *kusha* grass. The blood that flowed out turned to milk and the decapitated head told the prince that he, Nagarjuna, was headed for the Pure Land, but that he would be reincarnated and take birth again. Rattled, the prince moved far, far away from the body. It is said that each year, the head of Nagarjuna and his body move closer together, and when one day they meet, Nagarjuna will return to this earth to teach again.

He had also discovered the elixir of immortality, which he shared with his king so that both of them had the same lifespan. Thus, the king and his minister lived for many centuries.

The story is similar to the magical accounts of Nagarjuna found in Tibetan and Chinese tales.

Meanwhile, Tibetan biographies say that after Gautamiputra Satakarni died, his successor, the historical king of the Satavahana dynasty to whom Nagarjuna wrote *Friendly Epistles* (*Suhrlekha*), wished to appoint his own spiritual adviser, instead of inheriting Nagarjuna from his father, to better suit his preference for brahmanical beliefs. Instead of retiring him, however, the new king asked Nagarjuna to show compassion for him by committing suicide. Here too, the blade of holy grass was the chosen weapon, but this time, the story goes that Nagarjuna had accidentally uprooted it whilst creating a meditation cushion for himself. So, Nagarjuna was decapitated by a single blade of holy *kusha* grass.

The indisputable logic of both stories is that Nagarjuna, through his immense spiritual attainment, was in a position to choose self-willed death, brought about at a time and by a weapon of his own choice.

right
Naga princesses hold blazing wish-fulfilling jewels. Nagas are custodians of great wealth. Their palace roof is made of gold, auspicious corals and conch shells. The *Dzi* stones said to originate from Naga realms, are also depicted.

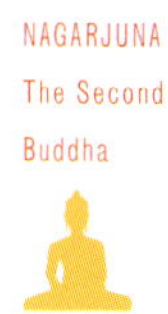

WORKS

I praise that perfect Buddha,
The Supreme Philosopher,
Who taught us relativity;
Free of cessation and creation,
Without annihilation and permanence,
With no coming and no going,
Not a unity, nor a plurality,
Fabrications quieted, the supreme bliss!

—MMK I, 1-2, tr. in Thurman

Had we been able to chart the life journey of Nagarjuna from the suckling baby destined to die within days to the legendary figure who may have lived for many hundred years and transformed Buddhism, his life would have been an inspirational example. Thankfully, there is more information available about his works, but even there, it's difficult to come up with an incontrovertible list of works. This is partly due to the tendency to attribute works to great scholars of the past. Thus, as mentioned earlier, four different Nagarjunas are believed to be the authors of pseudepigrapha.

left
Nagarjuna on a throne with the customary Nagas above his head.
A Naga offers him a manuscript.

The bīja of Nāgārjuna (8) is in the Shittan-shūji-ruijū.

The most famous of all the writings attributed to Nagarjuna is the *Madhyamakakarikas*, or *Karikas* as they are often called, a compilation of about 450 short stanzas divided into twenty-seven chapters. They address major philosophic issues such as the self, suffering and nirvana, causality and conditionality, and even the Buddha. Nagarjuna's profound insights altered the nature of the debate within Buddhism and made him a key figure in Mahayana Buddhism. But Nagarjuna's Sanskrit is dense and impersonal, as pointed out by David Loy. The *Karikas* were meant to be memorised and supplemented with an oral commentary by the teacher. Even then, Nagarjuna's philosophy is notoriously difficult to understand. He was a sceptic and some Buddhist practitioners question such philosophical investigations, focusing instead on prayer and meditation. However, Buddhism emphasises insight into the nature of the mind, which is usually trapped in thought patterns, and that is what Nagarjuna deconstructed. His radical approach does not, however, mean he was a radical, for his work was firmly rooted in the original teachings of the Buddha, who refused to discuss metaphysical questions. Instead, the Buddha compared his dharma to a raft, which should wisely be used to cross the ocean of life and death. Having crossed it, however, one should abandon the means used to get across. Nagarjuna had the same pragmatic approach to understanding the nature of the self, of the world, of suffering and nirvana.

According to Christian Lindtner, writings that can definitely be attributed to Nagarjuna are:

Mulamadhyamakakarika (Fundamental Verses of the Middle Way)

Sunyatasaptati (Seventy Verses on Emptiness)

Vigrahavyavartani (The End of Disputes)

Vaidalyaprakarana (Pulverising the Categories)

Vyavaharasiddhi (Proof of Convention)

Yuktisastika (Sixty Verses on Reasoning)

Catuhstava (Hymn to the Absolute Reality)

Ratnavali (Precious Garland)

Pratityasamutpadahrdayakarika (Constituents of Dependent Arising)

Sutrasamuccaya Bodhicittavivarana (Exposition of the Enlightened Mind)

Suhrlekha (Letter to a Good Friend)

Bodhisambhara (Requisites of Enlightenment)

The mantra for offering homage to Nagarjuna: *Om vajrabhasha rami svaha.* Vajrabhasa means master of transcendantal thought.

MULAMADHYAMAKAKARIKA

By Nagarjuna

Translated by Jay L Garfield

Based on the selection and arrangement by Rev. Yin Shun

1. I prostrate to the Perfect Buddha,
The best of teachers, who taught that
Whatever is dependently arisen is
Unceasing, unborn,

2. Unannihilated, not permanent,
Not coming, not going,
Without distinction, without identity,
And free from conceptual construction.

3. If all of this is empty,
Neither arising nor ceasing,
Then for you, it follows that
The Four Noble Truths do not exist.

4. If the Four Noble Truths do
not exist,
Then knowledge, abandonment,
Meditation and manifestation
Will be completely impossible.

5. If these things do not exist,
The four fruits will not arise.
Without the four fruits, there will be no attainers
of the fruits.
Nor will there be the faithful.

---

left
Nagarjuna in meditation.

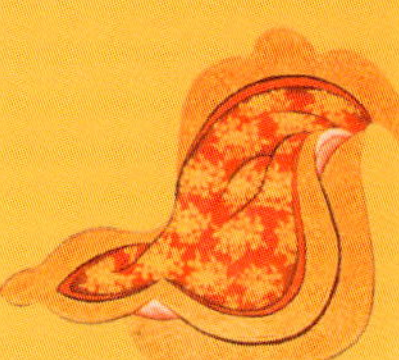

6. If so, the spiritual community will not
exist,
Nor will the eight kinds of person.
If the Four Noble Truths do not exist,
There will be no true Dharma.

7. If there is no doctrine and spiritual
community,
How can there be a Buddha?
If emptiness is conceived in this way,
The three jewels are contradicted.

8. Hence you assert that there are no real
fruits.
And no Dharma. The Dharma itself
And the conventional truth
Will be contradicted.

9. The Buddha's teaching of the Dharma
Is based on two truths:
A truth of worldly convention
And an ultimate truth.

10. Those who do not understand
The distinction drawn between these two truths
Do not understand
The Buddha's profound truth.

11. Without a foundation in the conventional
truth,
The significance of the ultimate cannot be
taught.
Without understanding the significance of the
ultimate,
Liberation is not achieved.

12. By a misperception of emptiness
A person of little intelligence is destroyed.
Like a snake incorrectly seized
Or like a spell incorrectly cast.

13. For that reason—that the Dharma is
Deep and difficult to understand and to learn—
The Buddha's mind despaired of
Being able to teach it.

14. Whatever is dependently co-arisen
That is explained to be emptiness.
That, being a dependent designation,
Is itself the middle way.

15. Something that is not dependently arisen,
Such a thing does not exist.
Therefore a non-empty thing
Does not exist.

16. For him to whom emptiness is clear,
Everything becomes clear.
For him to whom emptiness is not clear,
Nothing becomes clear.

17. If there is essence, the whole world
Will be unarising, unceasing,
And static. The entire phenomenal world
Would be immutable.

18. If it (the world) were not empty,
Then action would be without profit,
The act of ending suffering and
Abandoning misery and defilement would not
exist.

19. Whoever sees dependent arising
Also sees suffering
And its arising
And its cessation as well as the path.

20. Essence arising from
Causes and conditions makes no sense.
If essence came from causes and conditions,
Then it would be fabricated.

21. How could it be appropriate
For fabricated essence to come to be?

Essence itself is not artificial
And does not depend on another.

22. If there is no essence,
How can there be difference in entities?
The essence of difference in entities
Entities are established.

23. Without having essence or otherness
essence,
How can there be entities?
If there are essences and entities,
Entities are established.

24. If the entity is not established,
A nonentity is not established.
An entity that has become different
Is a nonentity, people say.

25. Those who see essence and essential
difference
And entities and nonentities,
They do not see
The truth taught by the Buddha.

26. The Victorious One, through knowledge
Of reality and unreality,

In the Discourse to Katyayana,
Refuted both 'it is' and 'it is not'.

27. The Victorious Conqueror has said that whatever
Is deceptive is false.
Compounded phenomena are all deceptive.
Therefore they are all false.

28. If whatever is deceptive is false,
What deceives?
The Victorious Conqueror has said about this
That emptiness is completely true.

29 If there were even a trifle non-empty,
Emptiness itself would be but a trifle.
But not even a trifle is non-empty,
How could emptiness be an entity?

30. The victorious ones have said
That emptiness is the relinquishing of all views.
For whomever emptiness is a view,
That one will accomplish nothing.

31. Desire, hatred and confusion all
Arise from thought, it is said.
They all depend on
The pleasant, the unpleasant, and errors.

32. Since whatever depends on the pleasant and the unpleasant
Does not exist through an essence,
The defilements
Do not really exist.

33. The self's existence or non-existence
Has in no way been established.
Without that, how could the defilements'
Existence or non-existence be established?

34. The defilements are somebody's.
But that one has not been established.
Without that possessor,
The defilements are nobody's.

35. View the defilements as you view your self:
They are not in the defiled in the fivefold way.
View the defiled as you view your self:
It is not in the defilements in the fivefold way.

36. Thus, through the cessation of error
Ignorance ceases.
When ignorance ceases
The compounded phenomena, etc., cease.

37. If someone's defilements
Existed through his essence,
How could they be relinquished?
Who could relinquish the existent?

38. If someone's defilements
Did not exist through his essence,
How could they be relinquished?
Who could relinquish the non-existent?

39. While this action has affliction as its nature
This affliction is not real in itself.
If affliction is not real in itself,
How can action be real in itself?

40. Action depends upon the agent.
The agent itself depends on action.
One cannot see any way
To establish them differently.

41. Emptiness and non-annihilation;
Cyclic existence and non-permanence:
That action is non-expiring
Is taught by the Buddha.

42. When asked about the beginning,
The Great Sage said that nothing is known of it.

Cyclic existence is without end and beginning.
So there is no beginning or end.

43. Where there is no beginning or end,
How could there be a middle?
It follows that thinking about this in terms of
Prior, posterior, and simultaneous is not
appropriate.

44. Some say suffering is self-produced,
Or produced from another or from both.
Or that it arises without a cause.
It is not the kind of thing to be produced.

45. If suffering came from itself,
Then it would not arise dependently.
For those aggregates
Arise in dependence on these aggregates.

46. If those were different from these,
Or if these were different from those,
Suffering could arise from another.
These would arise from those others.

47. If suffering were caused by each,
Suffering could be caused by both.
Not caused by self or by other,
How could suffering be uncaused?

48. If the self were the aggregates,
It would have arising and ceasing
(as properties).
If it were different from the aggregates,
It would not have the characteristics of the
aggregates.

49. If there were no self,
Where would the self's (properties) be?
From the pacification of the self and what
belongs to it,
One abstains from grasping onto 'I' and
'mine'.

50. One who does not grasp onto 'I' and
'mine',
That one does not exist.
One who does not grasp onto 'I' and
'mine',
He does not perceive.

51. When views of 'I' and 'mine' are
extinguished,
Whether with respect to the internal or
external,
The appropriator ceases.
This having ceased, birth ceases.

52. Action and misery having ceased, there is
nirvana.
Action and misery come from conceptual
thought.
This comes from mental fabrication.
Fabrication ceases through emptiness.

53. That there is a self has been taught,
And the doctrine of no-self,
By the buddhas, as well as the
Doctrine of neither self nor non-self.

54. What language expresses is
non-existent.
The sphere of thought is non-existent.
Un-arisen and un-ceased, like nirvana
Is the nature of things.

55. Everything is real and is not real,
Both real and not real,
Neither real nor not real.
This is Lord Buddha's teaching.

56. Not dependent on another, peaceful and
Not fabricated by mental fabrication,
Not thought, without distinctions,
That is the character of reality (that-ness).

57. Whatever comes into being dependent on another
Is not identical to that thing.
Nor is it different from it.
Therefore it is neither non-existent in time nor permanent.

58. By the buddhas, patrons of the world,
This immortal truth is taught:
Without identity, without distinction;
Not non-existent in time, not permanent.

59. That which comes and goes
Is dependent and changing.
That, when it is not dependent and changing,
Is taught to be nirvana.

60. The teacher has spoken of relinquishing
Becoming and dissolution.
Therefore, it makes sense that
Nirvana is neither existent nor non-existent.

61. Nirvana is said to be
Neither existent nor non-existent.
If the existent and the non-existent were established,
This would be established.

62. Having passed into nirvana, the Victorious Conqueror
Is neither said to be existent
Nor said to be non-existent.
Neither both nor neither are said.

63. So, when the victorious one abides, he
Is neither said to be existent
Nor said to be non-existent.
Neither both nor neither are said.

64. There is not the slightest difference
Between cyclic existence and nirvana.
There is not the slightest difference
Between nirvana and cyclic existence.

65. Neither the aggregates, nor different from the aggregates,
The aggregates are not in him, nor is he in the aggregates.
The Tathagata does not possess the aggregates.
What is the Tathagata?

66. One who grasps the view that the Tathagata exists,
Having seized the Buddha,

Constructs conceptual fabrications
About one who has achieved nirvana.

67. Since he is by nature empty,
The thought that the Buddha
Exists or does not exist
After nirvana is not appropriate.

68. Those who develop mental fabrications
with regard to the Buddha,
Who has gone beyond all
fabrications,
As a consequence of those
cognitive fabrications,
Fail to see the Tathagata.

69. Whatever is the essence of the Tathagata,
That is the essence of the world.
The Tathagata has no essence.
The world is without essence.

70. I prostrate to Gautama
Who through compassion

Taught the true doctrine,
Which leads to the relinquishing of
all views.

from left to right
Aryadeva, one of the two chief disciples;
Nagarjuna;
Asanga, the second chief disciple.

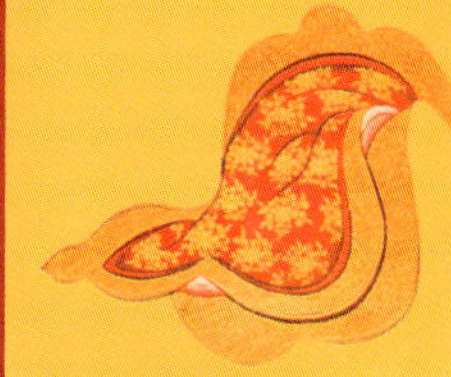

ETHICS

O King, it would be right for you
Each day to think about this advice
So that you and others may achieve
Complete and perfect Enlightenment.

—Nagarjuna

Nagarjuna's *Ratnavali* is not only counsel for a ruler on how to create social policies based on Buddhist beliefs but also a personal guide to one's conduct in life and on how to gain personal happiness. He explains the cause and effect of actions in ordinary human life and how meritorious, wise and compassionate deeds lead to freedom from suffering, the realisation of sunyata and the dawning of enlightenment. For the ruler, King Satavahana, Nagarjuna recommended a government that provided education and compassionate care for all living beings and he was against the death penalty. While it's hard to see how his recommendation to appoint government officials who are not seeking personal fame and fortune can be applied to our age, his penetrating analysis of reality, his description of ordinary life and the cause and effect that leads to release from suffering and progression towards buddhahood is still relevant today. In terms of the quality of one's soul and

left
Nagarjuna atop a tree with Bhavaviveka who studied his works at Nalanda.

nobility of thought and attitude as well as the ethics in the way one views ownership of property and possessions in the world, Nagarjuna deals with it all with compassion. The rejection of dogma and tolerance of Buddhism gives us the freedom to respect views that are not our own and creates space for an individual ethical compass and wise organisation of life and relationships. Whatever we do know about Nagarjuna indicates that he was an embodiment of virtue, possessing compassion and generosity in equal measure.

Sangharakshita's commentary on Nagarjuna's *Ratnavali* in his book *Living Ethically*, selections of which appear hereunder, sets out very clearly the ancient monk's advice. Sangharakshita, a British Buddhist scholar and former monk, explains in seven chapters Nagarjuna's counsel, given mainly within the framework of the five precepts for leading an ethical life.

1. Non-violence/Friendship: The Buddhist doctrine goes far beyond the basic injunction not to kill, extending it to not harming living beings, which includes hunting, i.e. killing animals for pleasure, violent films, pornographic films, terrorising others, and generally impeding the positive progress of others. Nagarjuna also covers the benefits of practising *metta bhavana* or kindness. Genuine *metta bhavana* towards others creates a spontaneous atmosphere of loving friendship, mental and physical pleasures and protection from violence. He discusses right livelihood, i.e. making a living by means that do not contradict the precepts, thereby excluding butchery, alcohol, weapons of war, jobs based on deception or dishonesty. Further, we should not waste our lives in positions we hate but should find something to do that will be an incentive to improving our performance and our lives.

2. Not Stealing/Generosity: Nagarjuna extends the second precept far beyond not stealing physical objects from others and suggests that we do not treat others as commodities. The ethical person does not violate others by manipulating them to advantage, robbing them of ideas or energies, or blocking their growth. He discusses the whole issue of give and take. In an ideal world, we would take only what we need and give what we can. However, present-day society is far from ideal; people worship money and greed is rampant, with maximum of the world's resources held in a few hands. People tread on each other to reach the top, they misappropriate ideas and possessions. A gift is not a gift if it is given with the intention to gain something in return because then it becomes merely a barter item. Gifts offered as undercover bribes in return for name, fame or fortune are not gifts at all. Nagarjuna's ideals include offering help out of a sense of love and not merely duty. There is great joy in helping others, both as individuals and as corporations. If the modern duty of CSR (Corporate Social Responsibility) is correctly followed, it will yield great dividends to the corporations. However, while we should make ourselves useful to others, we should not give unsolicited advice. Yet another quality that Nagarjuna stresses on, which is not very common today, is gratitude, a truly spiritual quality.

3. Sexual Relationships: The third precept, i.e. to abstain from sexual misconduct, is a difficult one to interpret for our age when sex has become an open subject in the public domain and sexual peccadillos rarely attract social censure. Sangharakshita interprets this precept in the broadest sense. Most obviously, it means not violating another for one's own sexual gratification. In our modern age, human trafficking, a trade currently worth about $30 billion annually, includes victims who are girls as young as four years of age and being raped daily in brothels. It also means not knowingly breaking up a marriage or other sexual partnership, and not to thoughtlessly misuse sexuality to achieve some other goal. Sangharakshita believes that in the contemporary world, romantic emotional attachment is more dangerous than sexual desire itself. It deludes us into projecting qualities onto the romantic partner that do not exist, causing people to feel bitter, lost and confused when the other person turns out to be different and the relationship breaks up. Most importantly, it is imperative to understand the effects of our sexual activity on our state of mind.

4. Not to Lie/Skillful Speech: Nagarjuna's *Precious Garland* elaborates at length on skillful and unskillful speech, which is not just about telling lies. While there can be a brief positive outcome from a lie, it is eventually discovered, and after that, our word will have little value. Malicious gossip, idle chatter, vile utterances designed to divide and create disharmony are to be shunned. In our modern age, politicians in democracies falsely claim that people do not want to be told the truth and use that as a shield for all kinds of chicanery and corruption. Skillful speech, on the other hand, should create harmony and be helpful to the other. Truth is paramount and it is important to tell the truth, even if it is sometimes painful. Equally, one should want to hear the truth, no matter how unpleasant, and listen without being defensive. Nagarjuna advises us to be open to hearing the truth and to act upon that immediately.

5. The Ethics of Views: This chapter provides the philosophical perspective for ethical practice. It focuses on the two false views, nihilism vs externalism. Nihilists assert that the world does not exist and that nothing remains of a person after death. Thus, they are averse to the world. Externalists take the world and life seriously but believe in a soul that continues to exist after death. However, that is not a positive mental state either, since it is based on attachment. According to Buddhists, neither of these views leads to liberation. Instead, existence is viewed as a process of flow and flux, wherein ever-changing mental states continue from this life to rebirth and so on. This chapter also addresses the negative effects of self-mortification and punishment, or drugs and alcohol and gambling. They will not lead to liberation. However, most of us find it difficult to follow the middle way of self-discipline and spiritual training.

6. Mindfulness/Mental States: Nagarjuna stresses the importance of being 'active and spontaneous and aware and mindful' all at the same time. For this, we must take daily stock of ourselves but Nagarjuna cautions against being too self-analytical or too spontaneous. *Precious Garland* lists fifty-seven unskillful mental states and how they affect our peace of mind, with instructions on how to cultivate contentment. He gives a thorough analysis of the forms of anger, pride, hypocrisy, flattery, jealousy and all the myriad small and seemingly trivial ways our minds stay attached, scattered or enmeshed in transitory phenomenon.

7. The Results of Actions: The law of karma can appear to be a nebulous and distant trend if we feel that it is spaced out over very many lives. However, Nagarjuna says that we are creating the world every moment by our character, our values, those whom we choose to associate with and how we treat them. There are very real consequences for our actions in this very lifetime. If we don't like the world we inhabit, we must realise that we are partly responsible for creating it and must work to change the conditions to create more positive mental states. While Nagarjuna believed in sacrificing a life of pleasure for future spiritual gains, Sangharakshita recommends enjoying pleasurable experiences as long as they do not contradict our spiritual life. Sangharakshita has done a great service by updating Nagarjuna's treatise to make it more relevant to our times. The question, it seems, we must ask ourselves at every moment is whether we are living more skilfully in consonance with the five precepts and Nagarjuna's clear guidelines to living more ethical lives.

Excerpt from the Paramitas:

Briefly the good qualities
Observed by Bodhisattvas are
Giving, ethics, patience, effort,
Concentration, wisdom, compassion, and so forth.

Giving is to give away one's wealth.
Ethics is to help others.
Patience is to have forsaken anger.
Effort is enthusiasm for virtues.

Concentration is unafflicted one-pointedness.
Wisdom is ascertainment of the meaning of the truths.
Compassion is a mind having one savour
Of mercy for all sentient beings.

From giving there arises wealth, from ethics happiness,
From patience a good appearance, from (effort in) virtue brilliance,
From concentration peace, from wisdom liberation,
From compassion all aims are achieved.

From the simultaneous perfection
Of all those seven is attained
The sphere of inconceivable wisdom,
The protectorship of the world.

page 62
A naga shades Nagarjuna as he sits peacefully with his hands in the Dharmachakra mudra. To his left is a stack of texts, which represents his written work.

THE PERFECTION OF WISDOM SUTRA

Nagarjuna brought the Prajnaparamita (Perfection of Wisdom), the outstanding collection of sutras, to the forefront of Buddhist thought and it also formed the foundation of his own Madhyamaka philosophy. Although the sutras are the teachings of the Buddha, they appeared to have been lost until Nagarjuna rediscovered them. While we have colourful legends of him recovering the texts from the Naga king's underwater domain, in truth, he may have recovered them from a tribe associated with Nagas (cobras): tantric tribes and practitioners are known to traditionally have 'abode of snakes' in their compounds. Nagarjuna is known to have gone on long pilgrimages, covering vast tracts of the country from the mountains to the seas, and could have come across the texts of the Buddha's sermons on transcendental wisdom on his wanderings.

Nagarjuna's Two Truths philosophy of the absolute truth and the conditioned truth indicates that the Absolute Truth is the deathless and changeless reality but it is not 'nothing'. The void too is void, but being unknown, human beings fear it, as they fear all that is unknown. Instead of engaging in futile metaphysical speculations, we are told it would be better to practise the dynamic virtues that will lead us, the individual, from sensual snares to enlightenment.

The Perfection of Wisdom sutras contain the short Heart Sutra and the Vajrachchedika (Diamond Cutter or Diamond Sutra). These two sutras, amongst the most popular in Mahayana traditions, expound that all beings, all dharma, all phenomena are empty (sunyata or void) of basic inherent existence.

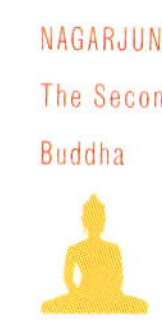

THE HEART SUTRA

May I be able to dispel the three poisons
May the light of insight shine brightly
May I be able to overcome all obstacles
May I be able to engage in the deeds of Bodhisattvas

—Barbara O'Brien

The Prajnaparamita Hrdaya, or Heart Sutra, is one of the most popular of Buddhist scriptures and is regularly chanted in Tibetan monasteries. Its Sanskrit title literally means 'The Heart of the Perfection of Transcendent Wisdom'. Along with the Diamond Sutra, it is one of the most prominent in the Prajnaparamita category in the Mahayana Buddhist traditions. The Heart Sutra is one of the shorter Perfection of Wisdom sutras with about fourteen Sanskrit slokas.

The Heart Sutra describes the experience of liberation of Avalokiteshvara, the Bodhisattva of Compassion, as a result of profound wisdom awakened in deep meditation. The insightful wisdom is the comprehension of the emptiness of all phenomena. Sunyata, or emptiness, in Buddhism, refers to the fact that nothing has ultimate immutable substance. Nothing has independent

left
The seven Nagas over the head of Nagaruna represting Shila-paramita, or transcendent moral behaviour.

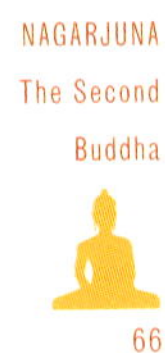

existence, nothing is permanent. Everything in the world is in a state of change and transformation. Understanding this leads to wisdom and cessation of suffering that comes from attachment of the ego to 'me' and 'mine', resistance to change, and grief over loss.

Nagarjuna said: 'The logs of wood which move down the river together are driven apart by every wave. Such inevitable parting should not be the cause of misery.'

In the Heart Sutra, Avalokiteshvara addresses Sariputra thus: 'Form is empty (sunyata). Emptiness is form.' The teachings are a statement expressing reality but the ultimate reality can only be experienced. Words are, at most, a second-best approximation of the supreme reality. The insight of wisdom refers to the inherent emptiness of forms, emotions, desires, thoughts and consciousness, i.e. the sum of a human being. Avalokiteshvara thus perceives reality without attachment. This perfection of wisdom is contained in the mantra at the end of the sutra.

The Heart Sutra

Translated by George Boeree

Avalokiteshvara, the Bodhisattva of Compassion, meditating deeply on Perfection of Wisdom, saw clearly that the five aspects of human existence are empty, and so released himself from suffering. Answering the monk Sariputra, he said this:

Body is nothing more than emptiness,
emptiness is nothing more than body.
The body is exactly empty,
and emptiness is exactly body.

The other four aspects of human existence—
feeling, thought, will, and consciousness—
are likewise nothing more than emptiness,
and emptiness nothing more than they.

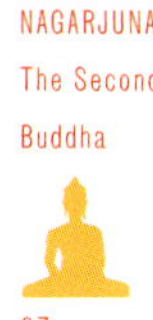

All things are empty:
Nothing is born, nothing dies,
nothing is pure, nothing is stained,
nothing increases and nothing decreases.

So, in emptiness, there is no body,
no feeling, no thought,
no will, no consciousness.
There are no eyes, no ears,
no nose, no tongue,
no body, no mind.
There is no seeing, no hearing,
no smelling, no tasting,
no touching, no imagining.
There is nothing seen, nor heard,
nor smelled, nor tasted,
nor touched, nor imagined.

There is no ignorance,
and no end to ignorance.
There is no old age and death,
and no end to old age and death.
There is no suffering, no cause of suffering,
no end to suffering, no path to follow.
There is no attainment of wisdom,
and no wisdom to attain.

The Bodhisattvas rely on the
Perfection of Wisdom,

and so with no delusions,
they feel no fear,
and have Nirvana here and now.

All the Buddhas,
past, present, and future,
rely on the Perfection of Wisdom,
and live in full enlightenment.

The Perfection of Wisdom is the greatest mantra.
It is the clearest mantra,
the highest mantra,
the mantra that removes all suffering.

This is truth that cannot be doubted.
Say it so:

Gaté, gaté, paragaté, parasamgaté.
Bodhi! Svaha!

Which means…

Gone, gone, gone over,
gone fully over.
Awakened!
So be it!

THE DIAMOND SUTRA

The Vajra Prajnaparamita Sutra is also known as the Diamond Sutra. *Vajra*, a Sanskrit word, means an indestructible substance, usually represented by a diamond. It alludes to the discourses on dharma. The Buddha, having spoken the Prajna for twenty years, declared that the Prajna sutras should be disseminated far and wide. The great Prajna Sutra comprises over 600 volumes, of which the Vajra Sutra is just one.

The Vajra heart is not the heart of flesh. The Buddha told Ananda that delusion is created by objects and impressions are caused by false thoughts, such as the thoughts that can transport us in an instant from England to Australia, from India to the sun and moon. *Vajra Prajna*, or *vajra* nature, is indestructible and able to cut through everything. The light of the *vajra* dispels the darkness of wrong dharma but is of 'no fixed dharma'.

'Sutra' can be interpreted as a bright revelation. Sutras also delineate a path to tread in life from birth to death.

'Paramita' means the sweetest of the sweet. *Paramita* is also a declaration in India when a task is completed to satisfaction.

left
Nagarjuna with Manjushri on the top right, as the Lord of Wisdom to destroy ignorance through the teaching of Prajnaparamita.

The Diamond Sutra

There are many translations of the Diamond Sutra. Here are excerpts of one of the translations by AF Price and Wong Mou-Lam:

Thus have I heard.

Once, the Buddha stayed at the Jeta grove in the kingdom of Sravasti, in the garden of Anathapindika (Benefactor of Orphans and the Solitary) together with 1,250 great *bhikshus*. It was the third assembly at the Jeta grove. He picked up his bowl and went to beg for food in the great city of Sravasti. On returning, he took his meal, washed his bowl, his feet and hands, and sat down nearby.

The venerable Subhuti rose from his seat, bared his right shoulder, knelt and addressed the Buddha respectfully thus:

'It is wonderful, World-honoured One, that the Tathagata thinks so much of all the Bodhisattvas and instructs them so well. World-honoured One, in case good men and good women ever feel the desire for Supreme Enlightenment, how would they abide by it? How would they keep their thoughts under control?'

The Buddha said: 'Well said, indeed, O Subhuti! Now listen attentively and I will tell you.'

The Buddha said to Subhuti:

'All the Bodhisattva-Mahasattvas should keep their thoughts under control. All kinds of beings such as the egg-born, the womb-born, the moisture-born, the miraculously born, those with form, those without form, those with consciousness, those without consciousness, those with no-consciousness and those without no-consciousness—they are all led by me to enter nirvana that leaves nothing behind and to attain final emancipation. Though beings immeasurable, innumerable and unlimited are emancipated, there are in reality no beings that are ever emancipated. Why, Subhuti? If a Bodhisattva retains the thought of an ego, a person, a being or a soul, he is no more a Bodhisattva.

'Again, Subhuti, when a Bodhisattva practises charity, he should not cherish the idea of a form when practising charity, nor is he to cherish the idea of a sound, an odour, a touch or a quality. Subhuti, should a Bodhisattva thus practise charity without cherishing any idea of form, his merit will be beyond conception. The merit of a Bodhisattva who practises charity without cherishing any idea of form; it is beyond conception.

'Subhuti, what do you think? Is the Tathagata to be recognised after a body-form?'

'No, World-honoured One, he is not to be recognised after a body-form. According to the Tathagata, a body-form is not a body-form.'

The Buddha said to Subhuti, 'All that has a form is an illusive existence. When it is perceived that all form is no-form, the Tathagata is recognised.'

Subhuti said to the Buddha: 'World-honoured One, if beings hear such words and statements, would they have a true faith in them?'

The Buddha said to Subhuti: 'In the five hundred years after the passing of the Tathagata, there may be beings who, having practised rules of morality and, being thus possessed of merit, happen to hear of these statements and it rouses a pure faith in them. Such beings, you must know, are those who have planted their root of merit not only under one, two, three, four or five Buddhas, but already under thousands of myriads of *asamkhyeya*s of Buddhas. Those, Subhuti, are all known to the Tathagata and recognised by him as having acquired such an immeasurable amount of merit. Why? Because all these beings are free from the idea of an ego, a person, a being or a soul; they are free from the idea of a dharma as well as from that of no-dharma. Why? If they cherish the idea of no-dharma, they are attached to an ego, a person, a being or a soul. Therefore, do not cherish the idea of a dharma, nor that of no-dharma. For this reason, the Tathagata always preaches thus: "O you *Bhikshu*s, know that my teaching is to be likened unto a raft. Even a dharma is cast aside, much more a no-dharma."

'Subhuti, what do you think? Has the Tathagata attained the supreme enlightenment? Has he something about which he could preach?'

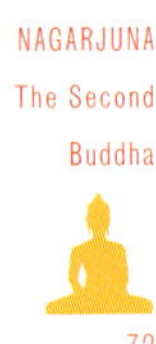

Subhuti said:

'World-honoured One, as I understand the teaching of the Buddha, there is no fixed doctrine about which the Tathagata would preach. Why? Because the doctrine he preaches is not to be adhered to, nor is it to be preached about; it is neither a dharma nor a no-dharma. How is it so? Because all wise men belong to the category known as non-doing (*asamskara*).'

The Buddha said to Subhuti: 'If there is a man who, holding even the four lines in this sutra, preaches about it to others, his merit will be superior because, Subhuti, all the Buddhas and their supreme enlightenment issue from this sutra. Again, Subhuti, wherever this sutra or even four lines of it are preached, this place will be respected by all beings including devas and asuras, as if it were the Buddha's own shrine or *chaitya*; how much more a person who can hold and recite this sutra would be revered! Subhuti, you should know that such a person achieves the highest, foremost and most wonderful deed. Wherever this sutra is kept, the place is to be regarded as if the Buddha or a venerable disciple of his were present.'

At that time, Subhuti said to the Buddha: 'World-honoured One, what will this sutra be called? How should we hold it?'

The Buddha said to Subhuti: 'This sutra will be called the Vajra Prajnaparamita, and by this title you will hold it.'

At that time Subhuti, listening to this sutra, had a deep understanding of its significance, and filled with tears of gratitude, said this to the Buddha: 'World-honoured One, it is not difficult for me to believe, to understand and to hold this sutra to which I have now listened; but in the ages to come, in the next five hundred years, if there are beings who, listening to this sutra, are able to believe, to understand and to hold it, they will indeed be most wonderful beings. Why? Because they will have no idea of an ego, of a person, of a being or of a soul. They are Buddhas who are free from all kinds of ideas.'

right
Nagarjuna with Aryadeva on his the bottom right, holding a manuscript of the Prajnaparamita.

The Buddha said to Subhuti: 'It is just as you say. If there be a man who, listening to this sutra, is neither frightened nor alarmed nor disturbed, you should know him as a wonderful person. Subhuti, long, long ago, when my body was cut to pieces by the King of Kalinga, I had neither the idea of an ego, nor the idea of a person, nor the idea of a being, nor the idea of a soul. Why? When at that time my body was dismembered, limb after limb, joint after joint, if I had the idea of an ego, or of a person, or of a being or of a soul, the feeling of anger and ill-will would have been awakened in me. Subhuti, I remember in my past hundred births, I was a rishi called Kshanti, and during those times I had neither the idea of an ego, nor that of a person, nor that of a being, nor that of a soul.

'Therefore, Subhuti, you should, detaching yourself from all ideas, rouse the desire for supreme enlightenment. You should cherish thoughts without dwelling on form, you should cherish thoughts without dwelling on sound, odour, taste, touch or quality. Therefore, the Buddha teaches that a Bodhisattva is not to practise charity by dwelling on form. Subhuti, the reason he practises charity is to benefit all beings.

'The Tathagata teaches that all ideas are no-ideas, and again, that all beings are no-beings. Subhuti, the Tathagata is the one who speaks what is true, the one who speaks what is real, the one whose words are as they are, the one who does not speak falsehood, the one who does not speak equivocally. Subhuti, in the Dharma attained by the Tathagata, there is neither truth nor falsehood.

'Subhuti, to sum up, there is in this sutra a mass of merit, immeasurable, innumerable and incomprehensible. The Tathagata has preached this for those who were awakened in the Mahayana (great vehicle), he has preached it for those who were awakened in the Sreshthayana (highest vehicle). If there were beings who would hold and learn and expound it for others, they would all be known to the Tathagata and recognised by him, and acquire merit which is unmeasured, immeasurable, innumerable and incomprehensible. Such beings are known to be carrying the supreme enlightenment attained by the Tathagata. Subhuti, wherever this sutra is preserved, there all beings, including devas and asuras, will come and worship it. This place will have to be known as a

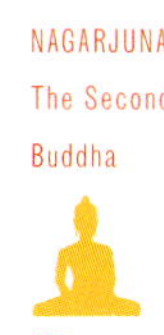

chaitya, the object of worship and obeisance, where the devotees gather around, scatter flowers and burn incense.

'Subhuti, as I remember, in my past lives innumerable *asamkhyeya* kalpas ago, I was with Dipankara Buddha, and at that time, I saw Buddhas as many as eighty-four hundred thousands of myriad *nayuta*s and made offerings to them and respectfully served them all, and not one of them was passed by, by me.

'If again in the last (five hundred) years, there have been people who hold and recite and learn this sutra, the merit they thus attain (would be beyond calculation), for when this is compared with the merit I have attained by serving all the Buddhas, the latter will not exceed one hundredth part of the former, no, not one hundred thousand ten millionth part. No, it is indeed beyond calculation, beyond analogy.

'Again, Subhuti, this Dharma is even and has neither elevation nor depression; and it is called supreme enlightenment. Because a man practises everything that is good, without cherishing the thought of an ego, a person, a being and a soul, he attains the supreme enlightenment.'

Then the World-honoured One uttered this *gatha*:

If any one by form sees me,
By voice seeks me,
This one walks the false path,
And cannot see the Tathagata.

'Subhuti, if a man should declare that the Tathagata is the one who comes, or goes, or sits or lies, he does not understand the meaning of my teachings. Why? The Tathagata does not come from anywhere, and does not depart to anywhere; therefore he is called the Tathagata.'

page 76-77
Naga princess hand over the Prajnaparamita to Nagarjuna while another Naga princess offers him homage with a bowl of fruits.

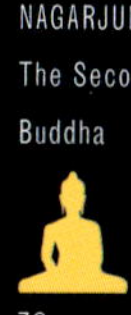

ACKNOWLEDGEMENTS

I acknowledge grateful thanks to the great scholars and seekers whose work has enabled me to meet the challenge of somewhat comprehending Nagarjuna's message and make my small offering to the stream of Buddhism: Professor Robert Thurman, Barbara O'Brien, Professor Jay Garfield, Professor George Boeree, Christian Lindtner, David Loy and *Tricycle: The Buddhist Review*, Paul Connelly, Sangharakshita, Pam Dodd and Windhorse Publications.

My sincere thanks to my dear friend Lord Professor Bhikhu Parekh, my mentor for many years, who critiqued several drafts of this book and made invaluable suggestions. I thank Aruna Vasudev for her faith, and for inspiring me to make the journey. And Dr Shomit Mitter for reading the manuscript. I thank my old friends for their encouragement. I also thank Shobit Arya, the publisher, for giving it his personal attention, and for the beautiful layout and illustrations.

You dwell among the causes of death like a butter lamp standing in a strong breeze.

—Nagarjuna

If a person is not earth, not water, not fire, not wind, not space, not consciousness, and not all of them, what person is there other than these?

A doer arises dependent on a doing, and a doing exists dependent on a doer. Except for that, we do not see another cause for their establishment.

By having faith, one relies on the dharma; by having wisdom, one truly knows. Of these two, wisdom is the chief; but faith is its prerequisite.

Just as the grammarian makes one study grammar, a Buddha teaches according to the tolerance of his students; some he urges to refrain from sins, others to do good, some to rely on dualism, others on non-dualism; and to some he teaches the profound, the terrifying, the practice of enlightenment, whose essence is emptiness.

—Nagarjuna